How to sell on eBay for beginners 2024

I0416741

Unlocking eBay's secret for novice sellers

JAKE HARRIS

How to sell on eBay for beginners 2024

How to sell on eBay for beginners 2024

Table of Contents

How to sell on eBay for beginners 2024

everything from vintage finds to cutting-edge technology.

One of eBay's key attractions is its inclusivity – everyone, from seasoned entrepreneurs to individuals cleaning out their closets, can find a place here. Whether you're selling handmade crafts, rare collectibles, or the latest gadgets, eBay provides a level playing field for sellers of all kinds. This inclusivity has contributed to the platform's vibrant and diverse community.

Meet Jake: Your Guide

Jake Harris, your guide on this eBay journey, has found success in the vast world of online selling. He promises a profitable and enjoyable eBay selling adventure, emphasizing a friendly, engaging, and achievable approach.

Navigating the eBay Landscape

Before we dive into the intricacies of eBay selling, let's reflect on your goals. What are you hoping to achieve by selling on eBay? Understanding your objectives will guide you in making informed decisions throughout your eBay journey.

Imagine a cluttered room filled with items you no longer use, taking up precious space and collecting dust. Jake found himself in this situation not too long ago. Wondering if there was a way to breathe new life into his forgotten treasures while making some extra money, he stumbled upon eBay – the

INTRODUCTION

Welcome to the exhilarating world of online entrepreneurship, where opportunities abound and success is just a few clicks away! If you're holding this book, you're about to embark on a journey into the dynamic world of eBay – one of the most vibrant online marketplaces globally. Congratulations on taking the first step towards unlocking the doors to a world of possibilities.

In this guide, we will unravel the secrets of selling on eBay for beginners, equipping you with the knowledge and strategies needed to navigate this digital marketplace successfully. Whether you're looking to declutter your home, start a side hustle, or build a full-fledged online business, eBay provides a platform where your aspirations can become a reality.

Why eBay?

You might be wondering, why eBay? What sets it apart from other online selling platforms? The answer lies in eBay's unique blend of accessibility, global reach, and diverse user base. Founded in 1995, eBay has evolved into a powerhouse of e-commerce, connecting millions of buyers and sellers worldwide. What started as a platform for individuals to auction off collectibles has transformed into a vast marketplace encompassing

How to sell on eBay for beginners 2024

So, find a comfortable spot, brew your favorite cup of tea or coffee, and get ready for an exhilarating journey. Whether you're a stay-at-home parent seeking extra income, a retiree in pursuit of a fulfilling hobby, or someone driven by a passion for entrepreneurship, this book is your passport to thriving in the dynamic eBay universe.

This is just the starting point of your expedition. Let's plunge into the vast world of eBay, tap into your selling potential, and explore the myriad opportunities waiting for you. Together, Jake and you will transform your dreams of online success into a vibrant reality.

HAPPY SELLING!

vibrant online marketplace that connects buyers and sellers from around the world.

Your Unique Journey

In the upcoming chapters, Jake will draw from his personal journey as a successful eBay seller to provide you with practical tips, tricks, and strategies. Starting from the very beginning, assuming no prior knowledge, he'll guide you through navigating the eBay marketplace. Together, you'll uncover the secrets of creating compelling product listings, capturing the attention of potential buyers, and maximizing your profits.

This guide is not just about the technical aspects of selling on eBay. It's an exploration of your creativity, an opportunity to nurture your entrepreneurial spirit, and an invitation to savor the excitement of building your own online business. Delve into buyer psychology, master effective communication, and understand the art of providing exceptional customer service that keeps customers coming back.

Throughout your shared adventure, Jake aims for you to feel empowered and inspired. Regardless of your background or experience level, eBay success is within your grasp. Selling on eBay allowed him to turn a passion for decluttering and a love for writing into a fulfilling venture. He believes it can do the same for you.

How to sell on eBay for beginners 2024

WHAT IS eBAY?

eBay stands as a pioneering online marketplace, serving as a global hub that seamlessly connects buyers and sellers. Founded in 1995 by American businessman Pierre Omidyar, eBay has evolved into a versatile platform where individuals and businesses can engage in the buying and selling of an extensive range of products. From electronics and fashion to collectibles and home goods, eBay offers a diverse marketplace catering to various interests and needs.

Headquartered in San Jose, California, eBay operates internationally, with individual sites catering to regions such as the European Union, numerous Asian nations, the United States, Canada, and more. The platform's user-friendly approach, coupled with its commitment to secure and open trading, has positioned eBay as a dominant force in the global e-commerce sector.

While initially known for its auction-style sales, eBay has expanded to include fixed-price transactions, catering to the varied preferences of its vast user base. Central to eBay's success has been PayPal, an online payment system that eBay acquired in 2002 and later split into a separate business in 2015. Notable acquisitions in the 2000s, including StubHub, Shopping.com,

Rent.com, and Skype (sold in 2009), further enriched eBay's offerings.

eBay relies on a feedback system, allowing users to grade sellers on transactions. This self-regulation mechanism aims to create a trustworthy trading community, although challenges and controversies have arisen. Despite facing legal pressures in Europe related to the distribution of counterfeit products, eBay has maintained a commitment to responsible business practices. Through the eBay Foundation, the company supports local community projects worldwide, showcasing its dedication to social responsibility.

WHY SELL ON eBAY?

In the ever-expanding landscape of online commerce, eBay stands out as a platform that doesn't compete with sellers, offering a secure alternative for brands and merchants. While Amazon serves as a formidable competitor, eBay's unique features and advantages make it a compelling choice for businesses looking to diversify their e-commerce strategies.

1. **Expand Your Audience:** With over 182 million active customers, eBay provides a

vast audience for brands and merchants. Selling on eBay allows businesses to tap into a different market segment and broaden their customer base.

2. **Examine New Regions and Markets:** International expansion can be costly and time-consuming. eBay simplifies this process by offering 25 international sites, enabling businesses to explore new regions without significant financial investments.

3. **Storefronts on eBay:** eBay Storefronts provide an excellent avenue for merchants to enhance brand recognition. It allows businesses to establish their brand identity within the eBay marketplace, providing a dedicated space for customers to explore products conveniently.

4. **eBay Fulfillment:** Managed Delivery, eBay's response to Fulfillment by Amazon, offers sellers a streamlined solution for storing, packaging, and shipping goods. This service reduces complexity, lowers costs, and enhances the overall level of service provided to customers.

In summary, eBay's unique position in the e-commerce landscape, coupled with its commitment to user-friendly practices, makes it an attractive platform for businesses seeking new opportunities and diverse markets. Whether you're a seasoned seller or just starting, eBay offers a dynamic and accessible space for online commerce.

BENEFITS AND OPPORTUNITIES OF SELLING ON eBAY

In the dynamic world of online commerce, eBay emerges as a platform offering a multitude of benefits and opportunities for both novices and seasoned entrepreneurs. Let's delve into these advantages:

1. **Global Reach and Extensive Customer Base:** eBay's unique strength lies in its capacity to connect sellers with a global customer base. With millions of users spanning the globe, eBay serves as a gateway for sellers to reach customers far beyond the confines of a traditional brick-and-mortar store.

2. **User-Friendly Interface:** eBay's interface is tailored for ease of use, making it accessible to sellers, regardless of their familiarity with online commerce. From the streamlined account setup to creating listings, eBay's intuitive design ensures a seamless experience with helpful tools and guides.

3. **Low Start-Up Costs and Flexibility:** Setting up shop on eBay requires minimal upfront investment, distinguishing it from conventional business models. This affordability allows sellers to commence on a smaller scale and expand gradually. Furthermore, eBay offers flexibility in terms of working hours, empowering sellers to manage their businesses at their convenience.

4. **Diverse Product Categories:** eBay accommodates an extensive array of product categories, ranging from electronics to handmade crafts. Sellers enjoy the freedom to choose products aligned with their passions or expertise, fostering a more enjoyable and personalized selling experience.

5. **Dynamic Pricing and Auction Format:** The auction-style format on eBay empowers sellers to optimize profits by allowing potential buyers to bid on items. The inclusion of the "Buy It Now" option facilitates fixed-price listings, catering to customers who prefer immediate purchases. This pricing flexibility enables sellers to adapt to ever-changing market conditions.

6. **Access to Analytics and Seller Tools:** eBay's suite of analytical tools equips sellers

with insights into performance metrics, customer behavior, and data-driven decision-making. These tools, complemented by features like promotional tools and seller protection policies, contribute to the growth and optimization of sellers' businesses.

7. **Thriving Community and Support:** Sellers on eBay become integral members of a vibrant community, fostering connections with experienced sellers and enthusiastic buyers. The platform's forums and discussion boards serve as valuable hubs for seeking advice, sharing knowledge, and gaining insights from the collective experiences of others.

HOW TO EFFECTIVELY USE THIS BOOK

Congratulations on selecting "How to Sell on eBay for Beginners" as your guide to embark on your eBay journey. To maximize the benefits of this resource, follow these steps:

1. **Read the Introduction:** Begin with the introduction to gain a comprehensive overview of eBay and grasp the potential opportunities that lie ahead.

2. **Sequential Learning Structure:** Progress through the chapters sequentially, starting from Chapter 2. Each chapter builds upon the preceding one, creating a logical and incremental learning experience.

3. **Note-Taking and Highlighting:** Record key concepts, strategies, and specific instructions while highlighting crucial points for easy reference.

4. **Actionable Tips and Examples:** Pay close attention to actionable tips and real-world examples embedded in the book. Implementation of these strategies will enhance your listings and elevate your chances of success.

5. **Active Implementation of Learning:** Actively apply the knowledge gained from

each chapter. Implementing strategies concurrently with learning accelerates your confidence and expedites positive results.

6. **Reference for Challenges:** Treat the book as a valuable reference guide. When faced with challenges or specific questions, revisit relevant chapters using the table of contents and index.

7. **Continuous Curiosity and Learning:** Recognize that eBay is a dynamic platform, necessitating ongoing learning. Explore eBay's resources, engage with online communities, and seek updated information to remain agile in the ever-evolving marketplace.

This book lays a solid foundation for navigating the eBay selling landscape. Embrace the learning journey, persist in your efforts, and relish the experience of evolving into a successful eBay seller.

.

GETTING STARTED WITH eBAY

Congratulations on taking the first step toward becoming a successful eBay seller! In this chapter, we'll guide you through the process of signing up for an eBay account, providing you with the essential information needed to embark on your eBay journey. By the end of this chapter, you'll have a solid foundation to confidently navigate the eBay platform.

.

SETTING UP AN eBAY ACCOUNT

While creating an eBay account is a straightforward process, doing it correctly is crucial. Beginner sellers often lack the fundamental knowledge required to set up an eBay account, such as adding payment options and configuring shop policies. This lack of understanding can hinder their ability to make sales when they first start.

A well-established account instills trust in clients, showcases credibility, and allows seamless transactions. Let's get started.

How to sell on eBay for beginners 2024

PERSONAL AND BUSINESS ACCOUNTS

Upon signing up for a new eBay account, you have the option to choose between a personal and a business account. If you want to associate your business identity with your eBay store, a business account is the ideal choice. However, a personal account is suitable for casual selling. Either way, you can later switch your account type if needed. Here's how to create an account:

1. Visit the official eBay website and click on "register" next to the eBay sign-in button in the upper left corner. You'll be directed to the eBay "Create an Account" page.

2. Use the toggles next to the "Personal account" and "Business account" buttons to easily choose the account type you prefer. Fill in your details accordingly, including your first name, last name, and password for a personal account, or business name, password, username, and business location for a business account.

3. Click the "Create Account" button to complete the first step of creating an eBay account.

Pro Tip: If you already have an eBay account from previous purchases, consider using it for selling. Having a buyer feedback score on the account can enhance its trustworthiness.

How to sell on eBay for beginners 2024

SWITCHING TO SELLING

Activating your eBay seller account and unlocking all of eBay's features requires a few additional steps. Here's how to switch to your seller account:

1. Log into your account and select "My eBay" from the drop-down menu in the upper right.

2. Choose "Selling" from the menu, and you'll be prompted to provide additional information for your seller account.

3. Fill in details such as your country, address, city, state, postal code, and phone number. Ensure the information is accurate to avoid potential issues in the future.

4. Upon completion, you'll see the prompt "Welcome to your selling overview!" This marks the activation of your eBay seller account, and you can use the "eBay Selling Overview" to sell items or review sales data.

For regular eBay selling, consider activating the "eBay Seller Hub," a more modern version of the "eBay Selling Overview." Your eBay seller account must have at least one sale before you can activate the Seller Hub.

How to sell on eBay for beginners 2024

To find the eBay Seller Hub page, simply search for "eBay Seller Hub" on Google.

ADDING PAYMENT METHODS

Before you can commence selling on eBay, it's crucial to link your payment accounts. eBay allows you to deposit the money you earn into your account using various payment options. Additionally, eBay levies service fees on purchases, making it essential to have a linked payment method right away.

How to Add a Payment Option:

To connect your bank account or credit/debit card to eBay, follow the instructions below.

To connect your bank account or credit/debit card to eBay, follow these steps:

1. On the eBay homepage, click on "Hi Name!" from the drop-down menu where the sign-in button for ebay.com was located. Select "Account Settings."

2. Your location will change to the "My eBay" page. Confirm that you are on the "Account" tab.

3. Under "Payment Information," click "Continue" when you receive a "Welcome!" message.

4. Choose "Add payment option" from the list of "Payment options." Depending on your location, you may see choices such as "Credit or debit card" and "Bank Account."

5. Click "Continue," and your payment method will be added upon providing the necessary information.

Crucial point about PayPal

As of now, eBay no longer supports PayPal as a method of payment acceptance for sellers. This decision aligns with eBay's aim to generate more revenue by managing payments internally, allowing them to retain a portion of transaction costs. This transition also results in reduced fees for sellers, dropping from 15% to about 12.09%.

In 2024, having a bank or checking account is mandatory to set up Managed Payments and receive funds from eBay while paying fees.

LINKING YOUR PAYONEER ACCOUNT TO eBAY

To link your Payoneer account to eBay, follow these steps:

1. Click "Register now" under "eBay is managing payments" on the Seller Hub.

2. Re-enter your password, then click "Get Started" after carefully reading all the instructions on the following eBay page.

eBay will guide you through the process. If you don't have a Payoneer account, make sure to create one, as you'll be asked for your Payoneer account information during the process. Your request will be submitted upon completion.

3. Wait a few days. If all your information is accurate and your request is accepted, eBay will send you an invitation.

UNDERSTANDING eBAY'S POLICIES AND GUIDELINES

Understanding eBay's guidelines and policies is crucial for ensuring a pleasant selling experience. Familiarize yourself with the following important topics:

1. **Seller Standards:** Sellers must adhere to eBay's requirements, including delivering excellent customer service, providing accurate item descriptions, and ensuring quick shipment. Familiarize yourself with these guidelines to maintain a good selling reputation.

2. **Listing Policies:** eBay has rules specifying what can and cannot be sold. Check the list of forbidden and restricted products to ensure your listings comply with eBay's policies.

3. **Seller Fees:** Selling goods on eBay incurs costs. To accurately estimate costs and set prices, understand the fee structure, including insertion fees, final value fees, and any other optional expenses.

4. **eBay Charges and Fees:** Many new sellers undersell their goods and incur losses due to unawareness of eBay fees. While there are various fees, most are optional. The main fees include:

    - **Insertion Fees:** The cost to obtain more listings, with eBay allowing 250 free listings monthly. Additional listings cost $0.35 each.

- **Final Value Fees:** A fee for the final value of each item sold, typically $0.30 plus a percentage of the total sale price (up to 12.9%, depending on the category).

DEVELOPING A GOOD SELLER REPUTATION

Building a good reputation is crucial for success as an eBay vendor. Here are some pointers:

1. Write precise and thorough product descriptions, including item characteristics and condition. Be open about any issues.

2. Capture crisp, eye-catching images showcasing your items' quality.

3. Dispatch products promptly and securely. Use appropriate packaging materials and provide tracking information.

4. Respond quickly to messages and inquiries, communicating professionally and transparently.

CREATING BUSINESS POLICIES

Establishing business policies early is crucial for building a long-lasting, viable eBay selling firm. Policies inform consumers about critical details like return costs, shipment schedules, and payment preferences. Follow these steps to begin creating policies:

1. Search for "eBay Business Policies" on Google.

2. After reading the content, select the "opt-in" link. Click "Get Started" on the next page.

3. Choose "Create policy" from the drop-down menu to begin creating payment, refund, and shipping policies.

FINDING PROFITABLE PRODUCTS TO SELL

CONDUCTING MARKET RESEARCH ON eBAY

Extensive market research is crucial for finding successful goods to offer on eBay. Follow these procedures for successful market research:

- **Examining eBay's Popular and Trending Items:** Use eBay's Trending and Popular Items categories to identify goods in high demand or becoming popular. Pay attention to recurring product categories to discover lucrative niches.

- **Using eBay's Advanced Search Options:** Utilize advanced search options to focus your research on specific factors like category, condition, price range, and item location. These filters provide insights into competition, pricing patterns, and consumer preferences.

- **Examining Data from Completed Listings and Sales:** Study completed listings to determine market demand and assess how comparable goods have performed on eBay.

This data reveals market value, consumer demand, and potential profitability.

- **Finding Specialized Markets and Product Opportunities:** Look for specialized markets and opportunities to sell unique products. Niche sectors often have less competition, allowing you to stand out and potentially increase profit margins.

Remember, eBay market research is an ongoing activity. Stay updated on industry trends, adjust your strategy as needed, and position yourself for success as an eBay seller

PRODUCT DEMAND AND COMPETITION EVALUATION

Assessing product demand and competition is essential to finding successful items to sell on eBay. Follow the methods below to accurately determine product demand and comprehend the competitive landscape:

1. **Examining Market Trends and Product Demand:**

   - Analyze consumer trends and market trends to determine the demand for a product.

   - Monitor news from the industry, social media trends, and cultural influences on consumer choices.

   - Explore eBay's "Popular on eBay" section for insights into current customer preferences.

2. **Analyzing Seller and Competition Metrics:**

How to sell on eBay for beginners 2024

- Understand the competitive environment by examining competitor listings.

- Focus on pricing, product presentation, delivery options, and seller reputation.

- Study feedback scores, positive reviews, and top-rated seller status for insights into credibility and customer satisfaction.

3. **Using Selling Insights and Reports on eBay:**

- Utilize eBay's tools like Terapeak and Seller Hub for market research and analysis.

- Gain information on market demand, sales patterns, and average selling prices.

- Identify popular categories and understand pricing patterns with data-driven judgments.

4. **Utilizing External Tools for Market Research:**

- Consider additional market research tools like Google Trends, SEMrush, and Jungle Scout.

- Conduct in-depth price analysis, keyword research, competition analysis, and market analysis using external resources.

By employing these techniques, you can gather insightful information to help you choose products to sell on eBay. The next section will cover various approaches to product procurement

SOURCING PRODUCTS FOR SALE

After determining lucrative products and evaluating market demand, the next step is to source items for eBay sales. This section will guide you through several sourcing strategies and considerations:

1. **Comprehending Various Sourcing Techniques:**

   - Wholesale: Purchase goods in large quantities at a discount from producers or wholesalers.

   - Dropshipping: Work with vendors handling inventory storage and client shipping on your behalf.

   - Retail Arbitrage: Purchase discounted goods from retail establishments or clearance sales for resale.

   - Local Sourcing: Explore garage sales, yard sales, and thrift shops for unique items.

   - Private Labeling: Develop your brand and have items produced under it for sale on eBay.

2. **Examining Regional and Online Wholesalers:**

   - Research local and online wholesale providers in your chosen product area.

   - Attend trade exhibitions, check wholesale directories, and contact manufacturers for potential suppliers.

   - Ensure vendors have a good reputation and consistently deliver high-quality goods.

3. **Examining Options for Dropshipping and Fulfillment:**

   - Explore reliable dropshipping vendors catering to your target market.

   - Consider third-party fulfillment facilities or services like eBay's Managed Payments for inventory storage and shipping.

4. **Making Use of Product Sourcing Tools and Apps:**

   - Utilize tools and applications like SaleHoo, Oberlo, or Inventory Source for monitoring inventory and discovering suppliers.

   - Compare costs and expedite the sourcing process using technology.

5. **Determining the Authenticity and Quality of a Product:**

- Ensure items meet strict standards for authenticity and quality before listing on eBay.

- Investigate products and suppliers thoroughly, read customer reviews, and request samples if necessary.

By exploring these sourcing options and considering item reliability and authenticity, you can create a trustworthy and diverse inventory for eBay sales.

The next section will cover understanding listing formats and product categories on eBay.

UNDERSTANDING LISTING FORMATS AND PRODUCT CATEGORIES

Understanding how product categories and listing formats operate is crucial for selling items on eBay. The following list of important factors and suggestions for raising awareness and sales will be your guide:

Exploring the Product Categories on eBay

How to sell on eBay for beginners 2024

To make it easier for customers to explore and locate what they're searching for, eBay categorizes its items into several groups. Learn about the categories and subcategories that are accessible and that apply to your items. This will make sure that potential buyers can find your ads with ease and in the proper location. To learn how vendors offer their items, look through comparable listings in the categories you've chosen.

Choose the Correct Category for Your Products

For your items to be seen and to reach the correct customers, you must choose the suitable category. Spend some time learning about and comprehending the eBay category hierarchy. As they may influence how customers search for and filter results, take into account the features and filters that are offered within each category. Consider the tastes and expectations of your target market when selecting the category that best describes your product.

Making Listings More Effective for Various Listing Formats

eBay provides a variety of listing forms, including fixed-price listings and auction-style listings. When deciding how to list your items, be aware of the benefits and factors to take into account for each format. While fixed-price ads give consumers the ease of rapid purchase, auction-style listings may elicit excitement and competitive bidding. Choose a format that reflects both the demand for your items and your pricing plan.

Recognizing the Value of Keywords and Product Descriptions

Write enticing and accurate product descriptions that highlight the essential characteristics, details, and advantages of your goods. In order to increase your descriptions' exposure in searches, use pertinent keywords. Think about the keywords that potential customers could use to find comparable items, then organically include those terms into your listings. Avoid employing incorrect or irrelevant keywords because doing so might turn off customers and damage your reputation.

Using Product Specifics and Attributes to Increase Visibility

Use eBay's product features and specifications to give in-depth details about your items. Buyers may filter and restrict search results using these details depending on specified criteria, such as brand, color, size, or condition. Fill out these fields completely to guarantee that your listings show up in pertinent searches and improve your chances of luring potential purchasers.

You may increase the visibility of your listings and draw in customers by comprehending eBay's product categories, picking the appropriate listing formats, optimizing your descriptions with pertinent keywords, and offering thorough product details.

CREATING COMPELLING PRODUCT LISTINGS

HOW TO CREATE A MAGNETIC TITLE

Do all in your power to pack the 55 permitted characters in the headline of your listing with well-known keywords that are also pertinent to the thing you're selling.

Naturally, this will comprise the product's title or name, its condition (if it's new), and any other terms that are frequently associated with your goods.

Make sure they are obviously pertinent to the product as well. Your title should include terms a customer could generally enter into an eBay search bar to find that sort of item because most buyers merely type in keywords when looking for products on eBay.

Stunning Listing Pictures

How to sell on eBay for beginners 2024

All of your listings' photographs have to be clear and polished, with a backdrop that contrasts with the color of the item. Most of the time, depending on the item being sold, you'll want to have many photos with each photo being shot from a different perspective and/or distance.

Never utilize a stock image from a manufacturer or dropshipper's website when you're selling a used item since it suggests that the item is brand new. You should take unique photographs of each object you own, whether it is brand-new or worn. A digital camera with at least 8 megapixels is best. A good image or two may do the majority of the selling for you, so make sure it's extremely simple to understand precisely what the item looks like from your picture(s).

METHODS FOR CHOOSING A STARTING PRICE

eBay advises all sellers to open their auctions with modest beginning bids, often between 1 penny and 99 cents, to promote bidding, draw buyers to the listings, and increase your visibility in the search results. Overpricing is one of the major errors that eBay sellers make, and those merchants rarely succeed.

Therefore, be careful to properly study your things before purchasing them. Also keep in mind that over 50% of eBay products often sell better at set prices as opposed to during auctions. Naturally, it's also essential to make sure your pricing is reasonable compared to those of other vendors who are currently offering the identical item.

Additionally, I advise you to always state that you welcome Best Offers (you don't have to accept any offers; nonetheless, you should still permit buyers to submit them since it shows you are adaptable and prepared to make concessions).

FORMATTING THE DESCRIPTION OF YOUR EBAY LISTING

Depending on the product being sold, descriptions might vary significantly, but generally speaking, every description should at the very least include everything listed below (often in this order):

More Advice

Text should be broken up into tiny, "bite-sized" chunks since extended paragraphs cause readers to tune out.

Give each component in the description a distinct structure, such as a header, brief paragraph, image, bullet-point list, brief paragraph, and policy information (contact, payment, shipping, returns, etc.), with enough of space between each one.

Use many distinct text colors, font sizes, and a font style that complements the item you're selling. Make your description entertaining to read and aesthetically appealing, in other words.

Generally speaking, it's better to use colors that complement the template you're using (see below).

Never use the standard font size, color, or style on a white backdrop instead of the default black! This makes it clear to potential customers that you spent very little time and effort writing your description.

LISTING TEMPLATES FOR eBAY

Always include a template, backdrop, or border in your listing that coordinates with the kind of goods you're offering and the color scheme of the description's content. Even if you continue to only use eBay's Selling form, you can add a Listing Designer template for 10 cents and pick from a wide variety of themes eBay offers:

A header that restates the product's name in a sizeable typeface, maybe bolded, underlined, or even all capitals, and that is printed in a standout color like dark blue or red. Most of the time, you can just restate your title.

A succinct, opening paragraph (no more than three phrases) outlining the product you're offering, its primary advantage, and its special features.

a picture of the goods that is accurate, complete, and well-done in the item description.

Additionally, you want to provide a list that is either bulleted or numbered, with brief, succinct

How to sell on eBay for beginners 2024

sentences that highlight the most crucial information and the item's selling aspects.

The primary advantages of buying this item might then be summarized in a second paragraph (optional).

Include areas for your refund policy, shipping information, and a contact section before you leave.

How to sell on eBay for beginners 2024

INCREASING LISTING VISIBILITY WITH SEO AND KEYWORDS

Welcome to the digital battleground of eBay, where increasing your listing visibility is the key to conquering the cutthroat online market. Elevate your eBay game by mastering the art of Search Engine Optimization (SEO) and strategically infusing your listings with captivating keywords. Here's your guide to not just surviving but thriving in the competitive world of eBay:

1. Conduct Keyword Research:

- Dive into the minds of potential buyers by conducting extensive keyword research.

- Explore the vast eBay landscape using the search box, uncovering popular and trending goods.

- Unearth hidden gems with third-party keyword research tools, revealing high-traffic, low-competition terms.

2. Include Keywords in Titles and Subtitles:

- Harness the mighty power of eBay's search algorithm by weaving pertinent keywords into your titles and subtitles.

- Craft titles that are not just informative but also magnetic, grabbing readers' attention from the first glance.

- Your title should not just tell but sell, effectively conveying the unique selling aspects of your product.

3. Optimize Your Product Descriptions:

- Transform your product descriptions into compelling narratives, rich with information and intrigue.

- Sprinkle keywords organically throughout, making sure to avoid the keyword overload pitfall.

- Every word should contribute to a vivid portrayal of your product, making it both visible and irresistible.

4. Use Item Specifics:

- Dive deeper into the specifics, utilizing eBay's dedicated sections for brand, model, size, and color.

- Infuse these fields with precision and detail, ensuring your listing stands out in eBay's search results.

- Keywords here are not just labels; they're the secret sauce for boosting your listing's visibility.

5. Utilize eBay's Promotional Tools:

- eBay equips you with an arsenal of promotional tools—promotions manager, markdown manager, and eBay deals.

- Strategically deploy these tools to create a buzz around your goods, attracting a swarm of eager buyers.

- Craft promotional content that not only appeals but also resonates, laden with captivating descriptions and strategic keywords.

6. Monitor Listing Performance:

- Venture into the realm of analytics, analyzing click-through rates, conversion rates, and sales statistics.

- Uncover patterns and ride the data wave, tweaking keywords, titles, and descriptions based on your audience's preferences.

- Your listings are dynamic—let them evolve based on real-time insights.

7. Optimize for Mobile:

- As mobile devices take center stage in the shopping arena, ensure your listings are mobile-friendly.

- Craft titles, descriptions, and images that dance gracefully on smaller screens.

- Embrace mobile-centric SEO tactics, serving up shorter headlines and succinct descriptions for an on-the-go shopping experience.

8. Ensure a Great Customer Experience:

- In eBay's realm, reputation is king. Uphold yours by delivering top-notch customer experiences.

- Let good feedback, prompt shipment, and stellar customer service be the pillars that elevate your visibility.

- Your commitment to excellence echoes in the visibility of your listings.

Stay nimble, adapt to eBay's ever-evolving rules and best practices, and watch your listings ascend to new heights in visibility, setting the stage for success.

THE MANAGEMENT OF SALES AND CUSTOMER SERVICE

Brace yourself for the eBay arena where success hinges not just on products but on the delicate dance of efficient sales management and top-tier customer care. Dive into the following pointers, and discover the art of not just selling but creating a shopping experience that customers will rave about:

MANAGING CUSTOMER COMMUNICATION AND INQUIRIES:

1. **React Quickly:**

   - Speed is your ally—respond to messages and queries within 24 hours, showcasing your dedication to stellar customer service.

2. **Be Respectful and Professional:**

How to sell on eBay for beginners 2024

- Let courtesy be your language, addressing customers by name and providing comprehensive responses.

- Your professionalism should resonate in every interaction, making customers feel valued and heard.

Give Specific Information:

- Enlighten customers with clear and accurate information about your products, shipping procedures, and any other pertinent details.

- Turn each interaction into an opportunity to guide customers towards making informed purchase decisions.

Provide Multiple Communication Routes:

- Open the gates wide—give customers various avenues to reach you, be it eBay messaging, email, or the good old phone.

- Be a maestro in the symphony of communication, responding promptly to each channel.

ORDER PROCESSING AND ITEM SHIPPING:

Processing orders quickly and properly is essential for adhering to your stated handling time and eBay's requirements for quick shipment.

1. **Dependable Packaging:**

   - Safeguard your treasures with packaging that not only protects but also showcases your commitment to quality.

2. **Give Tracking Details:**

   - Transform uncertainty into confidence by providing tracking numbers for each order.

   - Elevate the customer experience by keeping them in the loop, reducing the need for delivery update inquiries.

Considerations for International Shipping:

- Navigate the international seas with clarity—know the rules, customs, and any additional costs.

- Illuminate the path for overseas customers, ensuring a smooth and transparent shopping experience.

REFUNDS AND RETURNS MANAGEMENT:

1. **Declare Return Procedures Clearly:**

   - Let clarity be your beacon—declare return details in your ads, covering deadlines, conditions, and any applicable costs.

2. **Handle Returns Promptly:**

   - In the realm of returns, be swift— respond to requests with clarity, guiding customers through the process.

3. **Deal Professionally with Issues:**

   - Embrace problems as opportunities— professionally respond to unsatisfied customers, offering solutions that reflect fairness.

   - Your commitment to resolution echoes in the records you keep— detailed and transparent.

DELIVERING TOP-NOTCH CUSTOMER SERVICE

1. **Go Above and Beyond:**
   - Elevate your service to an art—send personalized thank-you cards, unveil exclusive deals, and offer a wealth of information.

2. **Take Initiative:**
   - Let your service be a dance, a rhythm of follow-ups that ensure customers not only buy once but return.

3. **Maintain Composure in Trying Circumstances:**
   - In the storm of customer complaints, be the calm—maintain composure, seek understanding, and find solutions.

How to sell on eBay for beginners 2024

- Let every criticism be a stepping stone to improvement, shaping a customer service experience that stands the test of time.

In the realm of eBay, where transactions are more than just exchanges, but experiences, your journey to success is paved with excellent customer service. Step confidently, adapt continuously, and let every interaction be a testament to your commitment to customer satisfaction.

DEALING WITH DIFFICULT CUSTOMERS: TURNING CHALLENGES INTO OPPORTUNITIES

Successfully managing sales and providing outstanding customer service involves navigating through challenging situations with customers. Here are some dynamic strategies for effectively dealing with difficult eBay customers:

1. **Maintain Your Cool and Work Smart:**

   - Always respond with professionalism and composure, avoiding reactions that may escalate the situation.

   - Cultivate empathy and try to understand the customer's perspective and concerns.

2. **Empathetic Responses and Active Listening:**

   - Actively listen to customer criticisms or concerns, allowing them to express themselves fully.

   - Address their issues with respect and empathy, reassuring them that their input is valued.

3. **Attempt to Comprehend and Clarify:**

   - Use open-ended questions to gain a deeper understanding of the customer's problem.

   - Paraphrase their concerns to demonstrate a thorough understanding and commitment to finding a solution.

4. **Offer Solutions and Options:**

   - Provide practical solutions to alleviate the customer's concerns and find a mutually agreeable resolution.

   - Be flexible and open to fair demands or compromises while adhering to your business constraints.

5. **Escalate When Necessary:**

   - If resolution seems challenging, consider escalating the matter to eBay's customer support or mediation services.

   - Provide a comprehensive description of the situation along with supporting evidence.

6. **Recordkeeping and Documentation:**

   - Keep thorough records of all communications with challenging clients, including texts, emails, and relevant paperwork.

- This documentation can be invaluable in case eBay intervention is needed.

7. **Maintain a Professional Public Image:**

- When facing challenges in a public forum, respond with courtesy and professionalism.

Offer a polite response to public complaints and extend an invitation to address the issue privately

AUCTIONS VS. FIXED PRICE LISTINGS: CHOOSING THE RIGHT SELLING STRATEGY ON EBAY

Choosing between auctions and fixed price listings is a strategic decision that impacts your eBay business. Each approach has distinct advantages and considerations:

1. **Auctions:** On eBay, auctions let sellers post goods with a beginning bid and a time limit for bids. When the auction time is over, bids

are placed, and the item is won by the bidder who placed the highest bid. Here are some advantages and things to think about while utilizing auctions:

Benefits:

- Encourages competitive bidding, creating excitement and potentially increasing the final selling price.

- Ideal for one-of-a-kind or rare items.

- Effective for clearance and liquidation of surplus stock.

Considerations:

- Uncertain final price.

- Time-consuming, especially when managing multiple auctions simultaneously.

2. **Fixed price listings:** With fixed price listings, vendors may specify a price for their products, and buyers can buy them right away at that price. Here some advantages and things to think about while utilizing fixed pricing listings:

How to sell on eBay for beginners 2024

Benefits:

- Provides control over pricing, ensuring predictable revenue for each transaction.

- Enables rapid transactions and appeals to buyers who prefer immediate purchases.

- Efficient for selling multiples of the same item.

Considerations:

- May lack the urgency associated with auctions.

- More challenging to stand out in highly competitive markets.

SELECTING THE EFFECTIVE APPROACH:

Take into account the following elements to identify the optimal selling strategy:

- Product Type: Auctions may be a better way to determine demand and value for rare or special things. For regular items with set prices, fixed price listings are suitable.

- Analyze the demand for your goods in the industry. An auction might assist increase the selling price if the item is highly sought-after. Fixed pricing listings could be effective for goods with steady demand.

- Auctions might be a smart move if you have extra inventory or need to swiftly get rid of products, according to inventory management. Fixed pricing listings provide you greater control and enable effective inventory management.

- Examine your pricing approach and decide if you like to set fixed prices or allow the market decide the value through open bidding.

- Consider your own preferences and the time you have available before choosing between managing auctions and fixed pricing listings.

Conclusion:

The decision between fixed price listings and auctions will rely on your goods, the state of the market, and your company's goals. Both methods offer advantages. When applicable, use both tactics to broaden your selling strategy and increase your success on eBay. Analyze the performance of your listings frequently to adjust your selling approach and catch up with shifting market conditions.

OPTIMIZING YOUR EBAY BUSINESS

Once you become an eBay seller, continuous optimization is key for success. Maximize efficiency, increase profitability, and grow your business with these strategies:

1. **Utilize eBay's Selling Tools and Features:**

   - Leverage resources like Seller Hub for unified management of listings, inventory, and performance data.

   - Explore promotional tools like the Global Shipping Program, Promoted Listings, and Seller Discounts.

2. **Explore Promotional Opportunities:**

   - Utilize unique deals, sales events, advertising mailings, and eBay campaigns to differentiate yourself and attract more customers.

3. **Implement Effective Inventory Management:**

   - Track stock levels, set low inventory alerts, and maintain accurate listings to prevent overselling or running out of products.

How to sell on eBay for beginners 2024

4. **Expand Your Business:**

   - Diversify your inventory and explore new product categories to attract a broader audience and increase sales potential.

5. **Optimize Customer Service:**

   - Respond promptly to customer inquiries, provide polite and efficient order processing, and go above and beyond to build trust and loyalty.

6. **Implement Efficient Pricing Tactics:**

   - Regularly assess your pricing strategy by monitoring market trends, competitors, and supply and demand factors.

7. **Stay Informed with eBay's Changes:**

   - Keep abreast of changes in services, policies, and algorithms by regularly checking eBay's seller announcements, emails, and policy updates.

8. **Review Performance Metrics:**

   - Regularly analyze sales statistics, conversion rates, and customer feedback to identify patterns, strengths, and areas for improvement.

9. Utilize Analytics Tools:

- Leverage third-party software or eBay's analytics tools to gain insights into customer behavior, popular items, and selling trends.

By consistently optimizing your eBay business, you can adapt to market changes and enhance your chances of sustained success

PREVENTING COMMON ERRORS AND PITFALLS

Selling on eBay can be a highly rewarding venture, but it's crucial to navigate the platform adeptly to avoid common pitfalls that might hinder your success. By understanding and proactively addressing these challenges, you can significantly enhance your chances of achieving your selling goals. Here's a closer look at common errors and tips on avoiding them:

INACCURATE OR INADEQUATE PRODUCT DESCRIPTIONS:

- Include complete and precise information about your products, covering aspects like condition, features, measurements, etc.

- Use clear, concise wording to ensure customers fully understand what they are purchasing.

How to sell on eBay for beginners 2024

IGNORING EBAY'S POLICIES AND STANDARDS:

- Familiarize yourself with and adhere to eBay's policies to avoid potential consequences such as account limits or suspensions.

- Stay updated on rules regarding prohibited goods, forbidden behavior, and seller expectations.

NEGLECTING HIGH-QUALITY PRODUCT IMAGES:

- High-quality visuals are essential for capturing customers' attention.

- Invest time in taking crisp, well-lit, and detailed pictures showcasing your items from various angles.

POOR COMMUNICATION AND CUSTOMER SERVICE:

- Timely and professional responses to buyer messages and inquiries are key.

- Act with courtesy, openness, and professionalism in all interactions to avoid misunderstandings and negative feedback.

FAILURE TO CONDUCT COMPETITIVE PRICING RESEARCH:

- Price your products competitively by conducting market research and comparing prices of similar items.

- Consider factors like quality, demand, and shipping costs when determining your prices.

POOR SHIPPING AND PACKAGING:

- Invest in proper packing materials to prevent shipping and packaging mistakes that can lead to damaged goods and dissatisfied customers.

- Adhere to eBay's shipping policies, use reliable delivery options, and provide accurate tracking information.

IGNORING CUSTOMER REVIEWS AND FEEDBACK:

- Customer reviews are valuable indicators of your performance.

- Pay attention to feedback, respond promptly and professionally to negative comments, and use feedback to enhance your offerings and customer support.

Neglecting Continuous Learning and Adaptation:

- Stay informed about eBay's policies, trends, and best practices.

- Regularly monitor and evaluate your listing's performance, and adapt your strategies to changing market conditions.

eBay is an active market that changes all the time. Your performance may be hampered if you are not current with eBay's policies, trends, and best practices. Keep yourself informed about new features, tactics, and tools that can help you enhance your selling abilities, optimize your listings, and adjust to market trends.

CONCLUSION: YOUR eBAY SUCCESS JOURNEY

Congratulations on completing this comprehensive guide to selling on eBay! We've covered the fundamentals of eBay selling, providing you with the knowledge and resources needed for successful use of the platform.

From understanding eBay's potential to finding profitable items, optimizing listings, managing sales and customer service, and avoiding common mistakes, you now have a solid foundation. The importance of continuous learning, adapting to market trends, and utilizing eBay's features for sellers has been emphasized.

Remember, success on eBay requires commitment, adaptability, and ongoing learning. Stay knowledgeable about industry trends, customer preferences, and emerging technologies to fuel your growth and profitability in this dynamic marketplace.

Engage with eBay's tools, communities, and forums to connect with fellow sellers, exchange insights, and gain valuable information. Beyond making sales, selling on eBay is about building relationships with your target audience, earning their trust, and establishing a robust brand. Success will follow your persistence, creativity, and enthusiasm for what you sell.

Thank you for joining us on this eBay selling adventure. We trust that this guide has equipped you with the knowledge and confidence needed to kickstart your eBay journey successfully. Happy bidding on eBay, and good luck with your endeavors!

www.ingramcontent.com/pod-product-compliance
Lightning Source LLC
Chambersburg PA
CBHW070957290526
45795CB00005B/1677